How I Met My Best Friend

![Dog on couch]

Jakes Journey

By

Cheryl Ann Whitsett

When my mommy met my daddy she wanted a dog so bad. He said when we get a house big enough we will get a dog. It seemed like an eternity.

Mommy and daddy bought a new house that is as big as the Empire State building. The back yard is fenced in and we (my girl and me) have a big place to run and play and a huge pool to jump in if we get too hot.

But enough of that. I have a great story because of my mommy…….

My name is Jake and I am almost 3 years old. I am a Labrador retriever mixed with Dalmatian. That is why I have pretty spots. I was adopted from the humane society as a puppy by an elderly woman. She didn't realize I was going to be a big boy, so she was going to return me.

Her granddaughter felt bad for me because I was a good boy so she looked for someone to take me so I wouldn't have to go back to the lonely place and listen to the dogs bark constantly. There is nothing worse than having to pee in your kennel in the same place you sleep.

The granddaughter found a friend that would foster me until someone would adopt me. His name was Chad. He had a dog and a cat. My skin was very red and itchy but he lost his job so he couldn't take me to the vet.

My daddy finally said mommy could get a dog. She went crazy looking on line at the humane society but she didn't see any dogs she liked. That's because I was over here waiting for her to pick me.

Mommy went on Craig's list and started looking at the dogs. Just so you know, people throw away their dogs for many reasons. Because they have to move and can't take their dogs with them, or have a baby, or they are too old or they don't have time for us. As a dog, I would just like to say, "Pets are forever". We would welcome your bundle of joy and be the baby's protector.

Daddy was home the night she was looking for a dog. It didn't have to be a puppy because mommy loved older dogs. She saw my picture and was in love with me. After all I am a dapper looking dude.

How could anyone not love me? Any dog that has a heart shaped nose is love. I was well behaved too. Mommy sent Chad an email and to another lady who had a German Sheppard. Chad called mommy the next day.

Boy they stayed on the phone for at least a half hour talking about me and Chad really was attached to me. Mommy could feel it. He said he would bring me to visit on Saturday to see if I was a good fit in mommy and daddy's home.

Saturday came and Chad said he couldn't bring me that day. Mommy was heartbroken. He said he had some things to do for his mom on Sunday and after that he would bring me over. Mommy was sad but was still hopeful.

I didn't really know what was going on but I got in the car and Chad told me he was taking me to meet some nice people. I was a little scared but he had taken such good care of me I trusted him. Oh his mom came too, to make sure they were good parents.

My daddy said "here comes our dog" when he saw me coming across the lawn. Mommy opened the door so fast and hugged me tight.

Daddy was a big goob acting like a little boy with his first dog.

I didn't know what was going on but my tail was wagging so fast mommy couldn't even get a picture of it.

I didn't know he was going to be my daddy or have a mommy just yet. Daddy took me outside in the back yard and I was like "cool dude you have a big yard". My tummy was upset from the ride so I flew down the side of the pool and made a huge pile of poop. Yep I did.

Mommy, daddy, Chad and his mommy were all standing around talking. He was happy and said he felt very comfortable leaving me here. I didn't know what that meant because I just thought I was going to visit.

Mommy gave him an autographed book and one to his mommy also. He told my mommy to take me outside until he left. Mommy knew this was so hard for him. He made mommy promise that she would keep in contact with him for at least a month and his mommy made her promise if she didn't want me, that I could call them and they would come back and get me.

Mommy was in love with me immediately. She said I was the next best thing to a million dollars. She went to pet smart and bought me a king size bed, lots of toys and some big treats. She already had food and a bowl for me to eat out of but I wasn't too hungry that night. When it was time for bed, mommy and daddy let me sleep with them. It was a rough night for me because I didn't know what was going on. Mommy whispered in my ear, "I am your new mommy now and everything is going to be perfect". I didn't know what happened to Chad he was gone. But I do know I felt super comfortable after mommy whispered in my ear. I laid in her arms all night. She even sang to me. I knew I could trust her.

In the morning when everyone got up, mommy let me outside and played ball with me. I was so happy to have a huge yard to play in and even a pool if I got too hot. You know us dapper dudes like to go skinny dipping.

Mommy is so loving and gives me a lot of kisses and hugs and always tells me I am a good boy and she loves me. I didn't really know what that kind of love was until my mommy and daddy came into my life.

They loved me from the beginning from a picture. Mommy said so.

I have many faces and names. Here I am a fortune teller and I told mommy her future is only love with me. She thinks I am the best fortune teller around.

I am the wolf in little red riding hood but I think a cool purple hoodie is awesome. Mommy says I look fly. A fly I was thinking but she meant I was super-duper cute.

I am the cutest dude on the beach with my sun glasses on. Mommy doesn't want the bright sun to hurt me so she put sunscreen on my delicate pink skin. I can't have my pretty spots all sun damaged. In the short time I have been with my mommy and daddy, I have found McDonald's cheeseburgers are so good, I love smoked bones preferably pork legs and mommy doesn't feed me cheap stuff. She said she will pay whatever she has to in order to keep me healthy.

Mommy took me to the vet a week after she got me. I had no records so the stupid vet had to give me all my shots again. I was a good boy, but my butt was sore as could be. At that visit I weighed in at 64lbs. The vet said that was a good weight. She put me on heart medication so I wouldn't have heart worms and gave mommy something for my itchy back side. The vet also gave mommy my microchip number so she could rescue me if I got stolen or went missing.

That is funny she doesn't know I would never go missing because I have the life now.

Mommy lets me sleep on her bed and she comes and rubs my head and tells me that she loves me all the time.

After she had me for six months I was due back at the vets. I weighed in at 84lbs and the vet gave my mom a hard time. She said she was going to put me on a diet but that went out the window quickly when my daddy comes home from work. He goes out for a long time but when he comes home I get to have table food. I am not a beggar I just sit and watch them eating and they give in. Because their food taste so much better than mine.

Mommy is a bit harder to get table food from. She doesn't give in too easily. Then she gets this bright idea to get me a play mate. She said if I had another dog to play with I would lose weight.

Mommy likes to cuddle with me in the bed. I think she thinks I am my daddy when he goes away for work. Sometimes I sigh and she knows I am fed up with her lol. I would never be fed up with mommy.

Mommy took me on an adventure to find a play mate for me. She took me to the Humane Society of Jacksonville Florida but then she left me in the office with these chicks that kept giving me treats.

I was kind of scared because I didn't want to stay here. Mommy wouldn't do that anyway. She was gone for hours. Then she came and got me and took me to the play yard. Whatever that meant. She said I was going to meet a girl named Tinkerbelle. I looked up at her thinking why do I need a girl I am neutered.

We got to the play yard and I saw my dame strutting across the grass. She was quite the looker too. The lady let us smell at the fence gate and I was thinking what is your problem let my chick in to see me. This isn't prison.

At the shelter her name was Tinker. Mommy didn't want to change it too much so she named her Tinkerbelle. She is an American Bulldog pit bull mix. I didn't know if I could like a pit bull, after all people say such horrible things about them. But Tinkerbelle was so cute.

Here is my girl and me playing outside. I am on the left with my cute little black ring around my tail and Tinkerbelle is on the right. She has some issues because she was starved and abandoned. I will tolerate them for a while but then she has to behave.

She steals my food and bones because she never had any. Mommy gets us washed up at night before bed because she says we are the dirtiest dogs ever. We can't get on the bed unless we get washed up.

When mommy brought Tinkerbelle home we played a lot. I was so out
of shape I had to go inside. That chick has no turn off switch. She just
wants to play, dig big holes in the back yard and ruin mommy's flower
beds.

Mommy dresses me up in pajamas to go to bed but I don't know why she puts pink ones on me. She tucks me in all tight so I won't be afraid. I am very afraid of thunder and I get in mommy's bed and get under her pillow. I know I am a big dude but I hate loud noises.

We don't like our picture taken and I always look the other way.
Mommy thought she was being smart her and had treats in her hand.
Of course you see Tinkerbelle further in the front of me because she
thinks she is always first for everything. Mommy makes her sit because
she is a crazy girl.

She can't help it because she was abused. Abandoned, starved and
abused. Mommy's quest in life is to help as many animals as she can.

We have four cats, two snakes and two iguanas that were rescues along with Tinkerbelle and me.

Sometimes she gets on my nerves and I growl at her when she takes my things but then we start fighting. Growling is a big no no around Tinkerbelle. It's not her fault she doesn't like to get yelled at. I don't blame her but I am a good boy so no one yells at me.

Mommy plays around and gives me such good looks. I think I look kind of smart with her glasses on, but then she can't see. My mommy is a big goof. My daddy loves us a lot. When he comes home from work, we get so much attention.

Sometimes I get mad because Tinkerbelle always wants to steal the show so daddy will take me on long walks or car rides without her.

I have to say I have had a great life so far. I have a nice big house and a big yard to play in. Who knows what would have happened to me if mommy couldn't get a dog.

Daddy knew she needed protection from crazy people. You know the kind of crazy that want to kill you. I would die trying to defend my mommy and daddy.

Mommy says I am her best friend. I really love her a lot. I look at her and she just melts. She could never be mad at me because I am a handsome dude. A hefty dude but never-the-less handsome.

I am Jake and I am love!

Words from my mommy:

Many animals each year are abandoned, abused and have broken souls. The family they knew didn't want them anymore for many reasons that are not cool and end up in shelters. I am proud of the city I live in because we have a no kill status.

I am many of those who would have been returned if good people had not stepped up to make sure I didn't go back to the shelter. My husband and I hate animals who are thrown away like garbage and abused.

Pets are for life no matter what is thrown at you. There is always a way to keep your pets if you just get the help you need. Many shelters will help with food if you can't feed them and even with housing that will accept pets.

Jake is only one of few who were lucky enough to find a forever home. Some will never be that lucky. If you want a pet, you have to understand they are for life not just while they make you happy.

If you don't want a dog or cat to keep, you can always foster until someone adopts them. Foster parents are what keeps Jacksonville at a no kill status. People take in dogs and cats until the mega adoption event.

There are many hoarding situations where people mean well but then realize it's too many for them to handle. That is when shelters get on over load.

If you cannot adopt or foster, then make donations of food and blankets to your local shelter. They have very little resources and can use as much donations as they can get. If you can't donate or foster then go give some of your time to the shelter.

All the dogs need to be walked every day. Please don't shop adopt!

Jakes story turned out for the best but many don't.

Cheryl Whitsett is a eight times published author. She lives in Jacksonville, Florida with her husband Thomas. She loves helping animals and is a big advocate for them. Her goal is to educate people through her own animal books.

Other books written by this author:

Saving Tinkerbelle

How a Dinosaur Became a Princess

Dream to Awaken From Once Click of Death

A Dream of Death Forgotten

The Prevalence of Love

Debts of Life

True Cupid.

All of her books are available on Amazon and Createspace.

Her goal is to get the word out about animal abuse.

www.ingramcontent.com/pod-product-compliance
Lightning Source LLC
Chambersburg PA
CBHW060829290526
45792CB00005BB/1859